NATU...

T0011249

Why Do We Need BEES?

by Laura K. Murray

PEBBLE
a capstone imprint

Published by Pebble, an imprint of Capstone
1710 Roe Crest Drive, North Mankato, Minnesota 56003
capstonepub.com

Copyright © 2024 by Capstone. All rights reserved. No part of this publication may be reproduced in whole or in part, or stored in a retrieval system, or transmitted in any form or by any means, electronic, mechanical, photocopying, recording, or otherwise, without written permission of the publisher.

Library of Congress Cataloging-in-Publication Data is available on the Library of Congress website.

ISBN: 9780756575199 (hardcover)
ISBN: 9780756575144 (paperback)
ISBN: 9780756575151 (ebook PDF)

Summary: Does the buzzing of a bee make you want to run away? Well, those little insects do a lot more than sting! They help pollinate many plants. We wouldn't have honey without them. And we've learned a lot from the homes they build.

Editorial Credits
Editor: Ericka Smith; Designer: Kayla Rossow; Media Researcher: Svetlana Zhurkin; Production Specialist: Katy LaVigne

Image Credits
Alamy: blickwinkel, 10; Getty Images: Ashley Cooper, 24, SDI Productions, 5; Shutterstock: Andreas H, 9, Anthony King Nature, 11, BearFotos, 20, Carlos Aguilar Moncayo, 17, Dave Massey, 29 (middle), DerekTeo, 21, DMV Photography, 6, Dusan Petkovic, 22, EMstudio-Bonheurem (honeycomb background), cover, back cover, and throughout, Faith Forrest (dotted background), cover and throughout, Grandpa, 27, HeatherJane, 29 (bottom), Juergen Faelchle, 4, Kenishirotie, 26, Lapa Smile, 23, Lasantha Ruwan, 16, Lubos Chlubny, 28, MakroBetz, 14, maxstockphoto, 19, Menno Schaefer, cover, Mirko Graul, 12, paula french, 15, StudioSmart, 18, Thitisan, 7, Tom Wang, 25, VectorMine, 8, Yuttana Joe, 29 (top); Superstock: Minden Pictures/Albert Lleal, 13

All internet sites appearing in back matter were available and accurate when this book was sent to press.

Printed and bound in the USA. 5425

Table of Contents

Words in **bold** are in the glossary.

Plant Helpers

A bumblebee lands on an apple blossom. It walks over the petals and eats. It picks up **pollen**. Then it buzzes away. It leaves the pollen on the next flower. This helps the flower grow into an apple.

People, plants, and animals need bees. Bees help plants grow. Animals and people eat those plants. This makes bees an important part of nature.

All About Bees

Bees are insects that fly. There are more than 20,000 kinds of bees. They live on most continents. But they don't live in Antarctica.

Australia's teddy bear bee

Most North American bees are wild. They have always lived there. Honeybees have not always been in North America. People brought them from Europe in the 1600s.

Most bees live alone. They make nests in the ground. Other bees live in **colonies**. Only some of those bees build hives.

A bee has three main body parts. They are the head, the thorax, and the abdomen. It has six legs. Four wings help it fly. And it has five eyes!

head   thorax   abdomen

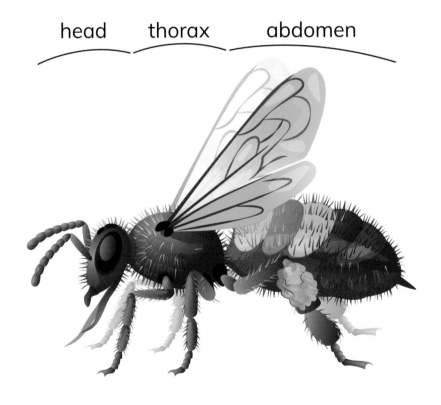

Bees are all different sizes. The smallest bee is less than 2 millimeters long! Wallace's giant bee is the largest bee. Its wingspan is 2.5 inches (6.4 centimeters).

Bees can be different colors. They can be colors like yellow, black, red, white, or blue.

Female bees lay eggs. In a honeybee hive, a queen bee lays eggs.

Some bees lay eggs in nests. Others lay eggs inside stems, logs, or twigs. They leave food. The young grow up on their own. In a colony, bees take care of the young together.

bee eggs

bees taking care of larvae

When bee **larvae** hatch, they look like small worms. They grow into **pupae**. Then they become adult bees. Some bees live a few weeks. Others live for years.

Only some bees sting. Male bees cannot sting. Some bees can sting only once. Others can sting many times.

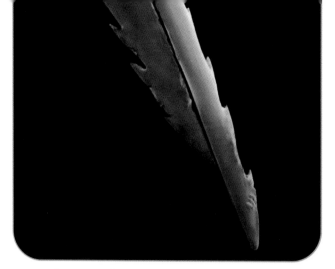

a honeybee's stinger under a microscope

Honeybees are more likely to sting than other bees. They do it to protect their hives. They have a **hollow** stinger. It has two rows of tiny blades. The bee puts out **venom** as it stings.

When a honeybee stings, it gives off chemicals. This warns the hive. But getting away after it stings **injures** the bee, and it dies.

How Do Bees Help Us?

Bees help with pollination. This is when pollen from the male part of a flower moves to the female part. Then the plant grows seeds or fruit. Bees pollinate 80 percent of all plants that have flowers.

How do they do that? Bees eat and gather **nectar** and pollen from plants. As they work, pollen sticks to them. When they move to another flower, the pollen rubs off.

Some bees have a special way to get pollen. They move their bodies very quickly. This shakes the pollen loose. Then the bee gathers it!

A lot of the world's food depends on bees. They pollinate crops like cherries and tomatoes. They also pollinate almond trees, lemon trees, and cocoa trees.

Bees also make food that humans eat. Honeybees make honey by gathering nectar. They bring it to the hive. Then they chew it. They pass it from bee to bee. They fan it with their wings. It becomes honey. Finally, they store it in their honeycomb.

People use honey, bee pollen, and beeswax for medicine and other products. Royal jelly is a milky liquid honeybees make. Some people use it as medicine.

A bee's venom can be useful to people too. Scientists are studying the use of bee venom to treat pain.

People also study bees' nests and
hives. It helps them design buildings.

Threats to Bees

People are a big threat to bees. They destroy the places where bees live and eat. Sometimes they spray harmful chemicals on plants to kill bugs. These **pesticides** kill bees.

Because of these activities, there are fewer bees today than there used to be. But people can help bees. They can grow flowers and plants that bees like.

Disease can destroy honeybee hives. People may worsen the problem by moving honeybees. Disease can spread easily.

Parasites harm bees too. Bee mites can kill bees. The mites feed on the bees. They can kill an entire colony.

Bee mites

Climate change is another threat to bees. It makes temperatures heat up. Plants might flower earlier. And bees might not pollinate them at the right time. Warmer weather also helps mites live longer.

A World Without Bees

Can you imagine a world without bees? Many vegetables, fruits, nuts, and flowers could disappear. Life would be harder for animals that eat those plants.

People might have less food too. Crops like apples, chocolate, and coffee could be hard to get. The price of food could go up.

People would have to find other ways to pollinate plants. Some people have already started to do it by hand. Others use robots or **drones.**

Bees are awesome! They are one of the planet's top pollinators. Humans, animals, and plants depend on them. Bees are an important part of nature we need!

COOL FACTS ABOUT BEES

- Leafcutting bees cut circles from plants and flowers to line their nests.

- A queen bee can lay more than 2,000 eggs per day.

- Cuckoo bees lay their eggs in nests built by other kinds of bees.

- The buzzing sound bees make comes from the fast beating of their wings. Some bees also buzz to shake pollen loose.

- It takes 12 honeybees their entire lives to make one teaspoon of honey.

- Bumblebees have fuzzy bodies to stay warm and fly in colder temperatures.

Glossary

climate change (KLY-muht CHAYNJ)—a significant change in Earth's climate over a period of time

colony (KAH-luh-nee)—a large group of insects that live together

drone (DROHN)—an unmanned, remote-controlled aircraft

hollow (HOL-oh)—empty on the inside

injure (in-JUHR)—to hurt or damage

larva (LAR-vuh)—an insect at the stage of development between an egg and an adult; more than one larva are larvae

nectar (NEK-tur)—a sweet liquid found in many flowers

parasite (PAIR-uh-site)—an animal or plant that lives on or inside another animal or plant and causes harm

pesticide (PES-tuh-side)—a poisonous chemical used to kill insects, rats, and fungi that can damage plants

pollen (POL-uhn)—tiny, usually yellow grains in flowers

pupa (PYOO-puh)—an insect at the stage of development between a larva and an adult; more than one pupa are pupae

venom (VEN-uhm)—a poisonous liquid some animals produce

Read More

Amstutz, Lisa J. *Fast Facts About Bees.*
North Mankato, MN: Capstone, 2021.

Caprioli, Claire. *A Swarm of Bees.* New York:
Scholastic, 2023.

Sang, Maivboon. *Bee Queens: Rulers of the Hive.*
North Mankato, MN: Capstone, 2023.

Internet Links

Britannica Kids: Bee
kids.britannica.com/kids/article/bee/352839

*National Geographic Kids: 10 Facts About
Honey Bees!*
www.natgeokids.com/au/discover/animals/insects/
honey-bees

Pest World for Kids: Bee Facts for Kids
pestworldforkids.org/pest-guide/bees

Index

About the Author

Laura K. Murray is the Minnesota-based author of more than 100 published or forthcoming books for young readers. She loves learning from fellow readers and helping others find their reading superpowers! Visit her at LauraKMurray.com.